# Christians and Demonology

## Stephen Anderson

## Rutherford House
## Edinburgh

Published by Rutherford House
17 Claremont Park, Edinburgh EH6 7PJ

ISBN 0 946068 58 5

# CUTTING EDGE

### A series of topical booklets
### tackling controversial issues

### SERIES EDITOR

### Graham Houston
### Chaplain to Heriot-Watt University, Edinburgh

# Contents

# Christians and Demonology

## Preface

This booklet has its origins in a paper presented to a conference of ministers at Crieff in January 1993 and was sparked off by teaching on two aspects of demonology from a group who previously had had little contact with Scotland. The two subjects were 'generational spirits' and 'the demonisation of Christians'. The latter subject especially has caused much controversy and some pain in Scotland over the last twenty five years and so I felt that the issues involved should be brought into the open. It is almost unnecessary to point out, however, that it will be impossible within the scope of this booklet to deal fully with these subjects. I can only hope to offer some pointers which I trust will be of help.

I am aware that we are all almost inevitably affected, if not conditioned, in our understanding and interpretation of Scripture by our own experience. Only too easily this can lead to an overemphasis in order to seek to redress an imbalance and to a stance which is polemic and leads to division and dissension.

The subject of demonic activity is prone to become a cause of division due to its very nature. However, as we examine 'generational spirits' and 'the demonisation of Christians' we need to recognise that neither of these subjects is, in itself, fundamental to the Gospel. They are not an integral part of salvation and as such we should be careful to allow liberty of opinion to others. It is however almost always in these areas of secondary and not prime importance that Satan seeks to cause division amongst those who are one in Christ.

The history of the Church abounds in examples of bitter feuds over secondary issues as the form of baptism, the nature of the communion service, and even the use of instruments to lead the praise in church services. We should therefore be very careful lest we fall into the trap of considering those who differ from us as being either inferior, in error, or not even Christians at all! So often the dogmatic positions taken up in these matters arise out of a basic insecurity and fear—if you are not too secure about something you shout the loudest!—and we need the humility to confess that we might not have all the truth. We need, too, to distinguish clearly between the truth of Scripture and the truth of our interpretation or experience of Scripture. Scripture will never be wrong but our understanding and our experience are, due to our fallenness, always suspect and capable of serious error.

I intend therefore to examine these two aspects of demonology and the Christian, but wider issues of spiritual warfare and biblical teaching on the forces of evil will need to be touched upon. My hope is that there will be a greater mutual understanding and tolerance amongst Christians so that we may share insights within the whole Body of Christ in order to enable the local Church (I would stress that this is the God-ordained agent) increasingly to meet the pastoral problems arising in these areas.

As we shall undoubtedly find, there is no straightforward scriptural solution to some of the problems raised in this field. Those with differing views will all claim biblical warrant to support their particular arguments. Furthermore, each view will cite experiences and case histories to support their positions. My prayer is that this booklet may help pastors and others to search the Scriptures diligently, to seek the help of the Holy Spirit and to find the truth as it is spelled out in Scripture. May we discover the balance of Scripture and use it circumspectly so that any line of teaching is accorded the appropriate weight which is given to it in the whole counsel of God. Then we may be enabled to bring the grace of Christ to bear in the pastoral situation to the glory of God.

# I

# Spiritual Warfare—Scriptural Balance

The very word 'balance' in the context of spiritual warfare may make some readers apprehensive. The word often seems to conjure up a suggestion of something static and evenly weighted so that there is equal choice between two sides. If that were the meaning such apprehension would be understandable but I use the word as I would of a gymnast or skier where balance is dynamic and imparts stability because there is no overemphasis to one side or the other. This clearly does not mean a balance between good and evil—the Christian must surely be totally and implacably opposed to evil in all its forms wherever it appears—but a balance in handling the Word of God as it deals with this difficult subject. Heresy and error are seldom a direct denial of truth but, just as evil can be a mere hairsbreadth deviation from good, so wrong thinking can be missing the mark—often by the veriest fraction—rather than shooting in the opposite direction.

Especially in the realm of this subject, an overstress can result in a teaching and experience which is tangential—starting in touch with the circle but gradually increasing its distance from the centre. We must seek to maintain a balanced biblical position by treating the divine revelations pertaining to our subject in the proportion which they occupy in the Scriptures.

For decades some sections of the Church, especially in the West, have undervalued the living Person of the Holy Spirit and discounted both angels and demons. The two seem to have gone together. Perhaps the blame must be laid at the door of the so-called age of reason or enlightenment where that which was not within the bounds of man's understanding came to be regarded as myth or superstition. Revelation was replaced by human reason as the ultimate arbiter of truth. As a result, the living God who acts was replaced by the 'inner being' of man or the concept of 'eternal Good' or some other phrase of anthropocentric thinking so that angels and demons (not to say the Holy Spirit himself) were dismissed at times with derision.

This imbalance has recently been in danger of being replaced with a counterbalance where even the reason of a mind renewed in Christ is discounted if not despised, with the result that demons are given unwarranted attention. To correct an imbalance with a counterbalance is never to achieve a balance. The pendulum then swings from one extreme to the other extreme only fleetingly touching the point of balance in the passing!

A recent publication carried the statement 'we are not to see demons everywhere'.[1] I enjoyed and appreciated the point being made. But has our understanding of this essential principle led us into a rationalistic view that demons are restricted in time and culture so that we can explain them away or ignore their reality in the West today?

We need to recognise the dangers of stressing the reality and activity of demons and many of these dangers will be spelt out in the pages that follow. However, two interconnected results are of such importance that they deserve mention at this stage.

First, humanity will be denigrated and degraded. Men and women, despite the Fall, are nevertheless created in the image of God and though that image is marred by sin, retain considerable divine qualities by means of general grace. Unlike the fallen angels they are redeemable and indeed will eventually judge angels (1Cor. 6:3).

Second, human responsibility and accountability before God will be reduced. To stress the grip of demons over a man encourages him to make excuses for himself and blame Satan for the unrighteousness in his life rather than admitting his own sin.[2] Each one will give account of himself to God (Rom. 14:12).

Perhaps too, we should take note that in Christian circles, the interest in spiritual warfare in recent years has increased in direct proportion to the interest in the occult in the secular world. There is a fascination with this whole subject as the popularity of Frank Peretti's novels amongst the Christian public bear witness.

Any open-minded reading of the Scriptures will reveal the importance they give to the spiritual warfare raging on this planet and the recognition by Jesus and the Apostles that this warfare involves not only Satan but also his demons or fallen angels or evil or unclean spirits.[3] To restrict this activity to New Testament times is, surely, to be highly selective in our treatment of Scripture and will mislead us as to what we should expect or indeed experience. The presence and power of evil spirits is certainly very familiar to peoples of other countries and cultures and well known to those working in Third World countries.

Many of us are becoming increasingly aware of the influence of the occult and the powerful effect upon young people of certain (clearly evil) computer games. Perhaps we are less aware of more subtle influences. A Christian psychiatrist writes; 'The influence of the occult especially on children is even more accessible than computer games—it is evident in children's TV and comics. I recently threw out a 'Disney' comic purchased by myself for my son because of clearly occult and New Age influences'.

One of the features of the modern Christian response to the occult has been the rise of particular people and groups claiming special gifts and ministries in bringing deliverance from spirits. Such a tendency leads almost inevitably to the cult of the individual and is suspect. Healing and dealing with demons are often associated in the Scriptures although not as often as some would have us believe. Healing in the Scriptures is normally referred to as a gift (*charisma*) and not a ministry (*diakonia*); see 1 Corinthians 12:28. In the same way the authority over demons was given to all the disciples as a gift. This ability is never listed amongst either gifts or ministries in the New Testament, but although it may well be that the lists are not exhaustive, we should be careful not to give it an unbiblical position of importance.

My own contacts with, and victories over, demons during the past twenty years have been in all the areas mentioned in the next chapter where I explain my involvement in this issue. But I would stress that I do not believe that I have a ministry in this sphere, and often wonder if I have a gift at all. Personally, I would far rather not become involved and I believe that such reluctance suggests an important principle: to get a name for a 'Deliverance Ministry' is a fearful responsibility.

When it comes to the issues of 'possession' are we 'keeping in step with the Spirit'? I suggest that many reformed and orthodox Churches are either spiritual ostriches with heads firmly in the sand or are, at best, like Gideon's men, 'faint but pursuing'! I also suggest that many charismatic Churches (especially para-Church organisations which often seem to adopt a more extreme attitude than the Churches) are in danger of switching the emphasis from the spiritual victory at Calvary to the spiritual battle today. Thus, whilst speaking of the battle being the Lord's, they show by their behaviour their confidence is in *their* ministry rather than in the Lord Himself.

I heard recently of a girl who had visited a centre where 'deliverance' was offered. She returned to her church without receiving any 'ministry', having been told that the only person in Britain who could help her was out of the country. I wondered where the Lord Jesus had gone!

Perhaps we all need to be reminded of the sovereignty of God in spiritual warfare as exhibited in physical warfare when David had reached the end of his tether. Apparently trapped in an impossible situation, David was only saved by the intervention of God by means of an unexpected Philistine raid on Israel which obliged Saul to break off the pursuit (1Sam. 23:26-8).

# II

# Spiritual Warfare—Areas of Attack

One of the greatest needs in the Church in these days of ever increasing spiritual confusion is for the gift of discernment of spirits.

The word used for this *discernment* or 'thorough judging' (*diakrisis*)[4] is unique in the New Testament and is used in 1 Corinthians 12:10. Unlike the other words used in the Scriptures for 'test' or 'try' or 'prove', *discernment* is in the context of the ministry of the Body or Church for the common good (1Cor. 12:7). Discernment indicates that thorough weighing of evidence which gives the 'ability to distinguish between spirits' (1Cor. 12:10, NIV). The ability follows the inward use of the gift.

The significance of the fact that these gifts are given within the Church can scarcely be overstressed. That the gifts are individually imparted is clear from the context, but that they are to be used in the context of building up the whole fellowship ensures that the one exercising the gift does so for the good of, and as a member of, the Body. The nose is vital for smelling but a disembodied nose would have no sense of smell: the ear is essential for hearing but disconnected from the brain it would be valueless. Scripture knows nothing of individualism.

What does this mean for today? Firstly that this gift of discernment must be recognised and acknowledged by the whole Church. The principle is the same as for prophets—they should be subject to the other prophets in the fellowship (1Cor. 14:32). This is a vital safeguard against those individuals who claim this gift and set themselves up—perhaps with a small group which they have gathered round themselves—to act as arbiters of spiritual matters. Such people are often of a forceful or charismatic personality and speak with considerable outward authority so that refutation is extremely difficult. Indeed, it is common for them to claim direct personal revelations from God so that to question what they say becomes to question God himself. The supposedly gifted individual, backed by his or her loyal or sycophantic supporters, will assume a spiritual assurance which will not only intimidate any who may have hesitations about the judgement made but may well lead into a spiritual pride with its attendant condemnatory and judgemental attitude towards those who do not agree.

We shall consider this in greater detail later but meanwhile I want to reinforce Michael Green's statement in his book *I Believe in Satan's Downfall* where he emphasises the need for much prayer and consultation with mature and wise Christians before leaping in 'where angels fear to tread'. If an individual feels a subjective call to exercise this gift without the backing of the Church, he or she is on dangerous ground. Similarly where a difficult case comes to light it is vital to consult with others and agree together in the Lord before taking action.

I return to the problems associated with those who claim and use this gift ill-advisedly. We shall consider later the harm that can be done in certain psychiatric cases but perhaps the most potent danger is that when the gift is used in an individualistic way it divides rather than builds up the fellowship. The individual (as opposed to the person who acts simply as a member of a fellowship) who discerns unclean spirits may end up accusing those who disagree with 'having a religious spirit' or of being occupied by an evil spirit. I speak from bitter experience over twenty-five years. We are to be careful about judging the hearts of fellow believers, (1Cor 4:5), and we should be aware that there is a thin line between feeling sad that a fellow believer has not shared our insight or experience on the one hand, and actually despising them on the other hand.

There may be disagreements in these areas and the assured individual is probably most dogmatic when he or she is feeling most insecure; in that case the gift will be exercised not in love but in an authoritarian attitude which purports to carry the authority of God. It is highly significant that the famous chapter on love is right in the midst of Paul's discourse on the exercising of spiritual gifts.

This is the first area of Satan's attack in spiritual warfare. To beguile believers into showing lack of love and thus causing division amongst God's children will be his way of seeking to hurt the very Heart and Spirit of God.

§

Before we go further into other main areas of attack we need to recognise the differences and interplay between the forces involved. These are sin, sins, and Satan or, as William Still has graphically put it, 'the root, the fruit and the brute.'[5]

Sin is evil which entered the universe from Satan through Adam (Rom. 5:12) and permeated all of humanity thus affecting the whole universe. That root of inborn and inbred sin finds its fruit in attitudes and actions of lawlessness (rebellion against the right and loving authority of God—1John 3:4) and frustrated failure to live as designed, (Rom. 3:23). Satan uses his influence over captive, fallen humanity to hide the Truth that sets sinners free and to give temporary satisfaction in the pleasures of self-gratification. In his attacks upon the believer he will seek:

- to undermine our faith, especially in the Word of God;
- to render us powerless by a sense of unforgivable guilt—he is the accuser of the brethren (Rev. 12:10);
- to lull us into a false sense of security (Jer. 6:14).

He works by these and other means to frustrate the purposes of God for believers which are that we may be holy and enter into our inheritance of salvation blessing in Christ.

If we fail to separate these three elements in the operation of evil we will fall into one of the ditches on each side of the narrow path. On one side, we will think of *sin* as sins rooted in our experience (either our own sins or those committed against us by others); consequently we will live defeated lives as we discover more and more failures within ourselves and in others, both in the present and in our memories. In other words, we will apply the Gospel to 'the fruit' rather than to 'the root' and will then be overcome by the constant reappearance of fresh 'suckers' springing up from the root itself.

The ditch on the other side is that of thinking too much of Satan so that we allow him to thrust his emphasis on failure, fear and self pity into that central position in our attitude and thinking which rightly belongs to the Lord Jesus and his love and forgiveness. This preoccupation with Satan denies and denigrates the dignity of men and women created in the image of God and can often be seen in the lives of those on the fringe of our mental hospitals. My Christian daughter was once firmly told that she was occupied by a demon of anxiety because she sat with her legs crossed. Only a healthy sense of humour (and proportion!) kept her from turning her eyes inward towards the supposed demon of anxiety and rather keeping them firmly upon Christ and her position in him as a princess of the Blood Royal.

If we need to discern between sin, sins and Satan we need also to discern between Satan and the Holy Spirit because his chief deception is to appear as 'the shining one' (the Hebrew word translated as serpent in Gen. 3:1) or as 'an angel of light' (2Cor. 11:14). While this is not a book on such discernment, certain principles may be of value.

1.  The Holy Spirit *convicts* (John 16:8); Satan *accuses* (Rev. 12:10). If conviction leads to confession then the Blood of Jesus cleanses from *all* sin (1John 1:5-9) and consequent accusation comes from Satan precisely because there is now no condemnation (Rom. 8:1, 33-4). His aim is to recreate the guilt Christ has carried away.
2.  The Holy Spirit speaks *in line with Scripture*; Satan casts *doubt*.
3.  The Holy Spirit upholds *order*; Satan introduces *confusion*.
4.  The Holy Spirit *points to the character of God* as revealed in Scripture, through the Lord Jesus; Satan *distorts that character* of holy love.
5.  The Holy Spirit *builds up* relationships among believers; Satan seeks to *introduce criticism and division*.
6.  The Holy Spirit is the *initiator of divine truth and grace*; Satan is the *counterfeiter*. C. S. Lewis writes: 'Goodness is itself; badness is only spoiled goodness. There must be something good first before it can be spoiled'.[6]
7.  The Holy Spirit says 'enter into victory *in Christ*; Satan says 'You can't, because...'

§

We now come to the some of the main areas of spiritual warfare as revealed in Scripture rather than deduced from Scripture.

## The Mind

In the context of spiritual warfare—arguments and false pretensions to frustrate the knowledge of God and his Truth—Scripture speaks of 'taking every thought captive to Christ' (2Cor 10:5). The picture is of Satan distorting the revealed knowledge of God. If only we would acknowledge it, he can be seen in nature:

> For since the creation of the world God's invisible qualities—his eternal power and divine nature—have been clearly seen, being understood from what has been made, so that men are without excuse (Rom. 1:20).

But he is fully displayed in the Word made flesh (John 1:14). Satan erodes the knowledge of God through arguments about the validity of the revelation and the nature of the divine Character, and through the proud setting up of a counterfeit alternative. Observe how Absolom followed a similar strategy when trying to usurp the throne from his father David (2Sam. 15:1-6). A correct attitude of mind, or biblically imbued thinking, as the base from which to refute and defeat Satan reflects the teaching of Jesus,[7] is a constant refrain in the writings of Paul[8] and is confirmed by the Apostle John[9] because it is as people think that they really are.[10]

This biblical thinking, 'the mind of Christ' or 'the mind of the Spirit',[11] is neither worldly wisdom nor intellectual ability but comes to the regenerate mind through a grasp of biblical doctrine, the key to which is obedience rather than IQ (John 7:17). After my conversion at the age of thirty-six I read very few Christian books and had never heard of a Bible commentary for the first three years but had read my Bible through about five times. At a conference when I spoke up in reply to an objection of the speaker to Scripture, I was accused of 'just following the IVF line'. I had to ask what IVF meant! The Spirit of God had used the Word of God to renew my mind and bring my thinking into line with sound doctrine.

It is significant that *truth* is the first article of the spiritual armour of God to be mentioned in Paul's picture of the equipment needed for spiritual warfare (Eph. 6:14). Truth, working in love, is vital because Satan, who is a liar from the beginning (John. 8:44), uses his lies to prevent fallen humanity from seeing the truth in Jesus (2Cor. 4:4). The denigration of doctrine and theology in many Christian circles today is highly disturbing and may, if unchecked, deflect the reviving movement of God's Spirit into Bypass Meadow.

## The Physical Realm

If the main battle is for the mind and takes place in the realm of thought and belief then we should expect Satan to attack in other ways which will affect right thinking. We are all aware of how physical weakness affects our minds and also how disturbing events can distort right thinking and attitudes. If we have paranormal experiences we are likely to think differently to the way we thought before. This is true whether the experience is a genuine spiritual experience or one induced by drugs or the occult.

Furthermore, it is generally accepted that major decisions should not be taken at times of stress such as bereavement or a broken relationship. We therefore need to see the opportunities for Satan to take advantage of the unwary in these three areas—

### Paranormal Phenomena

On occasion, paranormal phenomena may be a vehicle for demonic activity. I will give some examples:

- The haunting of people or places.
- The effect of cursing (but I am always encouraged by the ineffectiveness of Shimei and his curses upon King David (2Sam. 16:5-14).
- The activity of poltergeists.
- The activity of those imbued with supernatural strength by being demonised.

There are many other outward manifestations brought into the open by contact with the occult. This whole increasingly overt evil activity is probably on the increase because of the heightened image of the occult, although it may be that due to better publicity we hear more of such incidents than in the past. However, a detailed treatment of paranormal phenomena is outwith the scope of this book and can only briefly be touched upon.[12]

My own experience is that simple believing prayer using the authority of the Name of Jesus is totally effective in countering such activity. Moreover, I am persuaded that the paraphernalia of exorcism may often be a smoke screen erected by Satan to divert from the centrality and Lordship of Christ.

*Physical Health*

Again, an in-depth examination is beyond our scope here but the apparent increase in Satan's attack upon the health of Christian leaders and their families is significant. The rediscovery of the healing power of Christ through the Holy Spirit in many sections of the Church in recent decades has brought a new concentration of thinking upon the work of Satan in illness.

The simplistic view that all sickness is the direct result of sin or Satan's attack is scarcely in accordance with the teaching of Scripture and the distinction between ill health and demonisation is clearly shown in the ministry of the Lord Jesus. The table on the next page gives some illuminating figures. That certain illnesses are spiritually induced as well as being physical, psychological, psychiatric or psychosomatic is well attested in Scripture as well as being self-evident. This is a vast subject which we will only touch upon in succeeding chapters. Detailed study requires further reading. I would make a plea that readers select books by authors who start with the Scriptures and then move into experience rather than the other way round. Sometimes, one finds that Charismatic Catholics have been more faithful to Scripture than Protestant writers.[13]

| **Table** | | | | |
| | Record of miraculous healings in NT | Healing with no mention of demons | Demonised, separate from healing | Demonised, no record of symptoms | Demonised, with symptoms of illness |
| --- | --- | --- | --- | --- | --- |
| Gospels | 22 | 13 | 2 | 3 | 4 |
| Acts | 11 | 6 | 2 | 3 | 0 |

*Emotional Disturbance*

I am not primarily considering here past emotional hurts which are carried in the memory and may become fertile ground for Satanic attack. Much has been written on this subject and 'the healing of the memories' has become almost a specialist ministry. However, some of the methods used seem to have doubtful antecedents, for example, some are very similar to techniques used in voodoo. But clearly there is a great demand for biblical counselling for those suffering from emotional disturbance in these days of increasing stress and the alleged dramatic growth in child abuse.

In this section, I am mainly seeking to deal with those attitudes which are *both* spiritual and emotional. For instance we hear of a spirit of fear or of lust. We need to examine the meaning and choice of words carefully in this context but perplexingly a study of New Testament words used seems to indicate that the writers had the same problem as we do! The same word is often used for *spirit* and *emotion.*

What we call 'spirits' may be sin, emotion, or even a combination of both. For instance a 'spirit of anger' may well mean (and normally does) an emotion of anger felt by the person involved. Nor is this necessarily wrong as when Jesus deals with the merchants in the Temple (John 2:13-17). However, there is an anger which is sin, which is why the apostle says, 'Get rid of all bitterness, rage and anger' (Eph. 4:31), and the difference is clearly not between feeling and sin but between righteous and unrighteous anger. When our passions are aroused by anger, our attitudes are all too easily clouded by wrong emotion and therefore our judgements are distorted. Paul's words, 'In your anger do not sin' (Eph. 4:26), show that it is how the emotion is directed that determines whether it is good or evil.

Phrases such as 'a spirit of lust' which are not biblical but express a reality may fall into one of three categories:

- no demonic activity is involved—just human sin!
- the sin is aggravated by demonic activity.
- the sin is possibly caused by demonic activity.

In each case it is essential that the responsibility is placed firmly on the sinner.

Let me quote an example of how Satan can use the emotions to disrupt the Word and work of God. I was due to speak on the subject of 'The Devil' at a combined mission in Clydebank. As the prayer meeting immediately before the meeting was due to start, a young American on the team called David (who is now with the California State Police and built to suit) shared that he had had a dream that afternoon. In his dream three black hooded men had advanced up the aisle where he was sitting with the obvious intention of attacking the preacher. When asked what had happened he replied, 'I do not know. I tried to save you but was killed.' Some start to a meeting! Making sure that David was in no position to attempt any heroics, I went into Church knowing a very real grip of fear. It is on such occasions that one discovers the Biblical truth that the seat of the emotions is in the bowels!

During the singing of the first hymn, I knew with certainty that Satan, a liar from the beginning, had manufactured that dream in order to induce a paralysis of fear and so frustrate the free run of the Word of God. I interrupted the chairman, told the congregation the whole story, bringing the prince of darkness into the light of Christ and then prayed against him in the Name of Jesus. Fear was replaced by peace and the Lord spoke powerfully that evening.

There are, of course, other areas in which we could trace the activity of Satan. For example, much today is made of territorial spirits and the claiming of physical ground for Christ. But I suggest that if we examine the armour provided by God and described in Ephesians

6:14-18 we will recognise that the main attacks are likely to come in
the areas detailed above.

# III

# Demonology and Psychiatric Medicine

We have seen the clear distinction made in Scripture between the
healing of illness and the deliverance of the demonised. However,
the problem of distinguishing between the two in individual cases
remains with us today and presents real pastoral difficulties. Failing to make this distinction can lead to action which will worsen the
situation considerably. Perhaps this is especially true of Christians
who are psychiatric patients and we shall consider this in greater
depth when we ask whether Christians can be demonised (ch. 6). At
this stage in our discussion, there are a number of general points to
be made.

First, all healing and deliverance comes from God. There is a strand
of thinking which sees medicine in all its forms as *human* healing
and which restricts *divine* healing to the miraculous or apparently
miraculous. Such thinking stems from a total misunderstanding of
the nature of God and ignores the fact that medical means of healing
were by no means excluded in the New Testament.[14]

There is a tendency amongst certain 'spiritual healers' (many of
whom are inclined to combine healing activity with the casting out
of demons) to despise and even reject the medical profession. There
is also, of course, a reciprocal distrust, which tendency has been
highlighted in the recent BBC television programme 'The Healer',
although I must point out that the healer concerned in the play
made no profession of faith in Christ and never used his Name.

Second, we need to recognise the confusion that is often evident in
the attitude of Christians to mental illness. This is particularly so in
psychotic illnesses such as schizophrenia, when the individual may
express 'religious' and 'spiritual' delusions. These delusions tend to
be interpreted as demonisation rather than illness by Christians
who will then advise a spiritual cure rather than the more appropri-

ate and necessary medical treatment. It has been suggested over the years that those who think they are devil-possessed seldom are, while those who are possessed tend not to be aware of it.[15]

Third, we need to consider those cases of severe depression when a patient may experience delusions of profound guilt, inadequacy and failure or a sense of being beyond the reach of forgiveness, believing they have committed the unpardonable sin. A Christian suffering acute depression may doubt his or her salvation altogether. Here again medical treatment is necessary to alleviate the symptoms and restore a measure of rationality before the individual is able to respond to spiritual help.

Unnecessary distress is often caused to those, already suffering greatly as a result of illness, by well-meaning Christians who 'minister' to them by 'dealing' with the spirit of depression, implying that their condition, rather than being a genuine illness, is the result of a spiritual problem or failure. This is not to deny that the Devil does attack the physical and mental health of the Lord's servants and their families but even then treatment for the illness is necessary as well as the claiming of protection and liberation from the Devil's attacks.

§

This raises the problem of discernment between those who are genuinely demonised (see ch. 6) and those who may consider themselves demonised or behave as if they were, due to human psychological pressure.

There is a not insignificant group of patients with serious psychiatric disorders, usually schizophrenia or severe depression, who claim to be demonised. Sadly some Christians accept no distinction between a spiritual and physical (psychiatric) condition. One feature of such patients may be a craving for love and attention and this can lead to a display of all the classic symptoms being put on to attract such attention.

During a recent counselling session, the person concerned recognised that, by the assumption of the symptoms of demon possession, self-pity had caused the manipulation of many friends who had tried to help. There had clearly been demonic activity but not in the way in which it appeared on the surface and not as 'diagnosed' by those ministering. The casting out of these spirits had therefore been accompanied by the classic methods of exorcism but at a deeper level the patient was aware of the falsehood so that the real problem, which was self-pity, had never been dealt with.

A number of years ago a young woman was—I quote—'delivered of various demons'. As a result she joined a local Youth Fellowship and found herself very much the centre of attraction. After some weeks the interest in her waned somewhat. The symptoms of 'demonisation' reappeared and were duly cast out. Once again she was the centre of attraction. This vicious cycle continued with increasing regularity until she was faced with the truth about herself! Clearly her symptoms were self-induced as she struggled to find love and acceptance.

Behaviour and experiences, identified by some as demonic, may also be psychologically induced in a great number of ways. Secular psychiatric history is replete with examples of this in, for instance, the works of Mesmer and Charcot. Most Christian psychiatrists accept that some causes of such behaviour may fall into this category. Some cases of supposed casting out of demons may well come into one of these categories. We must first recognise that the outward symptoms will appear identical to those of genuine spiritual victories. Christians have really had the sort of experience where they 'felt the spirit getting stuck in my throat and then being coughed or yawned out'. Other Christians have witnessed similar phenomena. My concern is not to deny these things happen but rather to enquire as to the causes.

Intensive methods of (so-called) 'ministry' may be used, often late at night and sometimes, sadly, degrading to the dignity of a child of God. Such 'ministry' can be extremely powerful psychologically and those being treated are easily influenced by conscious or unconscious suggestions conveyed either at the time or from the past. In such cases the outward signs associated with deliverance can be reproduced by the human psyche, prompted by ideas formerly received from verbal or written teaching. If someone is expecting something to happen it is much more likely to do so, as hypnotists know only too well. I understand that hallucinations are almost invariably associated with previous expectations the one hallucinating may have had.

'Large group phenomena', including peer pressure and the manipulation (sometimes unconscious, sometimes deliberate) of emotions, often aided by skilful use of music or chants, are also very powerful. Such methods are surprisingly close to those used by Voodoo and ancient occultic rites. Their effectiveness has been proved over the centuries.

Consider also the use of undue pressure to get 'results'. This sometimes arises from a genuine desire to experience the Holy Spirit at work and see his blessing upon the person being ministered to. Alas, it can easily lead into undue human pressure which in turn can have unhappy consequences. Such pressure is in itself an indication of a lack of faith in the Holy Spirit. He can work long after you or I have left the scene!

Let us be sure that along with other Christians, we wait upon the Lord for his help in discernment and that we accept in practice, as well as in theory, that ultimate truth and authority rests in Scripture. We must always bring all our experiences to the touchstone of the Word of God, ever aware that Satan may operate either directly or more subtly through human psychological pressure. The enemy is the same but the means of victory are very different.

# IV

# A Third Force

Having expressed a degree of caution against an over-eagerness to find demons where the problem may lie in another direction, we need to stand firm upon the biblical position that there *is* a Devil and his demons are *real*. Many modern churchmen, as well as secular philosophers and psychologists, have suggested dismissive arguments which require to be refuted. Frank Lyall, Professor of Law in Aberdeen University, was a member of the Working Party on Parapsychology appointed by the General Assembly of the Church of Scotland in 1975. He submitted a paper from which I quote with his permission.

> 'For many the Bible itself is sufficient authority for dealing with the subject of exorcism, but there are also many for whom the very idea of demons and the notion of evil as a personality is abhorrent. We ought therefore first to consider shortly the arguments by which the NT accounts are commonly attacked. I select five; the argument from scientific advance; the limited knowledge of Jesus and the concealment of truth, which are variants on the same theme; dualism and the abrogation of responsibility by the 'invention' of the demonic realm. In doing this I seek not necessarily to convince, but to show that these common arguments are not final and cannot be relied on to dismiss the demonic.'

He develops persuasive arguments to demonstrate that although there can be little or no scientific proof for the existence of demons yet we must conclude that science here is neutral—'and the supernatural is unfalsifiable.' The only way out and forward is a step of faith. One has to choose between the Jesus of the New Testament and those theologians who deny the plain truth of what he said and did and who attempt to uncover and expound some 'hidden meaning'. The choice is both clear and crucial.

Any disagreements that may be expressed in this book about some of the current practices with regard to demonology are therefore not of the substance of the faith in demons! My contention is that problems arise because most of the practitioners in this area have little theological or biblical training. The result has often been to call upon Scripture to support experience. What I am convinced is required, both now and increasingly in the future, is a fresh look by those with a high view of Scripture at the activity of demons in our

Western culture. I do not believe that this has been done seriously and therefore we find ourselves floundering when we come to consider demonic activity. Let me say that I am grateful to many of those whom I may criticise who have been brave enough to get involved with demons.

If what follows reflects a bias against certain lines of teaching, I hope it will be understood that my comments arise out of many negative experiences over the last twenty years and that if some of my views are ill-advised I will be forgiven. My aim is to encourage a biblical and balanced entry into this difficult field by truly Bible-believing Christians who are learning to start with the Word of God.

Once again let me make a plea for mutual understanding between those who are in Christ. Are we honest and humble enough to admit that in some of our views we may be wrong without that admission damaging our faith? Of course we can only consider that Spirit-filled Christians can be wrong on minor issues if we rid ourselves of the notion that absolutes are now established in the lives of those who are both made perfect and are being made perfect (Heb. 10:14). I am referring to the view some hold that every idea and part of those who are redeemed sinners is either of God or of Satan. Such a view almost inevitably leads to the conviction that those who disagree with what they are convinced is of God are somehow affected to some degree by Satan. At the shallow end, they may consider them deceived; at the deep end, they may think of them as demonised.

To think in such terms makes humanity into puppetry and is an insult to the God who made men and women in his own image. To denigrate those God has made is ultimately to denigrate God. If this is true then we need to recognise that spiritual warfare is always a tripartite affair. A person is not merely the empty vessel in and through which the forces of good and evil wage war and battle it out. Each has responsibilities both of choice and of prayer and therefore may sometimes be seen as the 'third force'.

By 'third force' I mean that effective power over Satan and demons (and probably over certain illnesses) is not necessarily that of Jesus Christ. Remember Matthew 7:22:

'Many will say to me on that day, "Lord, Lord, did we not
prophesy in your name, and in your name drive out demons
and perform many miracles?"'

Neither can that power reasonably be of evil or else that kingdom
would fall.

'If Satan drives out Satan, he is divided against himself.
How then can his kingdom stand?' (Matt. 12:26).

Therefore it must lie within the potential of men and women themselves. Jesus cites 'Your people', evidently Jewish exorcists (*cf* Acts
19:13-16) who were, at least in some cases, operating successfully:

'If I drive out demons by Beelzebub, by whom do your people drive them out?' (Matt. 12:27).

His point is to show that such people were not working through
satanic powers. Yet it is clear that they were not empowered by the
Spirit of Jesus as is evidenced by the seven sons of Sceva (Acts 19:13-
16). Is there therefore a natural human ability able to take a stand
against evil powers?

I am indebted to Frank Lyall in this context who suggested in his
paper quoted above that these exorcists were able to use natural
powers as humans created in the divine image. Although marred in
every respect by the Fall, they were in the image of the all-powerful
God, designed to have dominion, to have everything put under their
feet,[16] and so were able to use natural powers to cast out evil spirits,
at least to a certain level. Professor Lyall again:

'First, a point which enthusiastic Christians often lose sight
of. Exorcism is not necessarily Christian for it to work. There
is, for example, much contemporary non-Christian faith-
healing, some of which uses exorcistic techniques. The power
to work miracles or exorcise is no guarantee of the Holy
Spirit. Jesus warns of many who will claim to have done
wonderful things in his name but in vain, (Matt. 7: 21-3).
Secular history of the time confirms the prevalence of exorcists in New Testament times'. (Lyall cites five authorities).

The question immediately arises, 'But how could non-Christian 'exorcism' work?' It seems to me that a distinction has to be drawn

between 'exorcism' done by the authority of Christ and that done by force of will. By the latter I mean that it could well be possible for an evil spiritual force to be driven out by the force of a stronger human will. We have no evidence that demons are bound to be stronger than we are. Indeed, we are told to 'resist the devil and he will flee from you' (Jas 4:7b). On this level, such a non-Christian exorcism (which might also be carried out by a Christian) is merely a matter of strength of purpose and force of will.

This leads me to suggest that the elaborate rituals by which some practise exorcism are not efficacious because of the rituals *per se*. Rather that the repetition of awesome names with the use of ceremonial (or whatever) is not a tool to drive out the demon but functions through its effect of harnessing and canalising the will of the exorcist. It could well be that the ceremonial serves to concentrate the will, making it more powerful than the will of the demon.

But there is a distinction between force (or power) and authority. Jesus makes that distinction in Luke 10:19: 'Behold, I have given you authority to tread upon serpents and scorpions, and to overcome all the power of the enemy'—a grant of *exousia* over the enemy's *dunamis*. Power and authority are connected in human experience in that occasionally authority has to prove itself by force; but usually force is not needed. Compliance is produced simply by the manifestation of authority, not by threat or compulsion. Our society runs on the basis of such authority, and so, in even greater measure, does God's Kingdom.

This explanation of a 'third force' seems to me to be eminently biblical. After all, believers are to judge angels, presumably fallen ones (1Cor 6:3). Perhaps part of the rage aroused against humanity in demons is because they know that even in their original state they were created to be messengers whereas men and women were created for a relationship of love with the Creator. My explanation seems, too, to give logical reasons for the apparent success of much faith healing and faith deliverance today. Note that I draw the distinction between 'faith' and 'divine' healing and deliverance.

The situation is certainly more complex than some would have us believe. This leads us into the two subjects where there is widespread confusion and where much sensitivity is required in pastoral situations: the issue of 'generational sin' and the question as to whether Christians can be demonised. We shall deal with each of these in turn.

# V

# Generational Sin

The ministry of deliverance has come into considerable prominence in recent years and such books as *Healing through Deliverance*[17] make two assumptions which are closely related. The first is that people with problems, including Christians, can be, indeed usually are, occupied by an evil or unclean spirit. Such an evil spirit has been (the argument goes) introduced into the family by sin, demonic activity or a curse in a previous generation and there is a carry over up to the third or fourth generation. This assumption and its consequences will be investigated in this chapter.

The second assumption is that Christians can be 'demonised', and we should note that, although the words 'demon possession' may not be used, the word 'occupied' frequently appears. This 'occupation' is understood to be either by spirits inherited from the past (as in the paragraph above), or by occult activity either before or since being regenerate by the Holy Spirit. Sometimes the word 'attached' is used and I can go along with that; it conjures up a biblical picture, often painted helpfully by William Still, of one of Satan's demons sitting on the shoulder of a Christian and whispering into his ear until he can become convinced the whispers actually come from within himself.

However, there is a world of difference between 'attachment' and 'occupation'. The latter conjures up in the mind the sense of something deep inside and therefore having to come (or be forced) out. 'Occupation' suggests something has somehow got beyond the barrier of God's Holy Spirit into his very temple, into the believer's inner soul.

I would like to offer a semi-theological critique of this assumption in the next chapter and then refer briefly to the practical and pastoral implications of such teaching. I do this (I trust) in humility, and certainly with considerable diffidence since those who hold this position are Christian people and it is not my intention to be judgemental. I write because I believe that there are serious misunderstandings and that God wishes to release his people from any error which takes away from the liberating truth of our Lord Jesus and his finished work.

Returning to the question of what is known as generational sin it is significant that this teaching has been held by the founders of most of the sects which have arisen this century. The basis of this view is that the sins of the fathers are visited upon the children up to four generations (Exod. 20:5). This is the key verse on which the doctrine is based. Other supporting biblical references are normally either parallel passages to the second commandment which will be covered in our investigation below or else are verses understood to be relevant although a straightforward reading of them in their context does not suggest such an interpretation.

We shall note four points with regard to the principle drawn from the second commandment because it seems to me that the exegesis is basically flawed and if the teaching is based upon a flawed understanding of Scripture then the whole doctrine is most certainly highly suspect.

1. The statement in Exodus 20:5 has to do with punishment from God and not the opening of a person to evil spirits. If God has decreed this punishment, we should be very wary of going against him by seeking to 'deliver' the sufferer. Denis Sutherland has commented helpfully:

> 'Ex 20: 5 is not about either the transmission of sin or of demons. It is about punishment. We are responsible for our own sins and are generally not punished for those of others. This, however, is a special case. In the OT the punishment for idolatry nationally was to be dispossession and the ap-

propriation of the land by enemies. Where this took place
(at the decree of God) it would take the family and the na-
tion three or four generations to recover even if all the
descendants were godly. I do not deny that characteristics
and specific sins (or perhaps weaknesses in the areas of
certain sins—SNA[18]) can be passed from parent to child
(although insufficient allowance is made for nature). Exodus 20:5 is not about hereditary transmission'.

2. The verse is more of a warning of consequence than a threat
because the judgement of God in punishment is always a 'strange
act' (See Isa. 28:21 AV: '...that he may do his work, his strange work;
and bring to pass his act, his strange act.')

3. The warning is attached specifically to the second commandment because of the devastating effect of idolatry upon God himself
and his people. It may be argued from Exodus 34:6f that the principle is widened but in context this verse refers to a renewed covenant
following upon the idolatry of the golden calf:

And he passed in front of Moses, proclaiming, 'The Lord,
the compassionate and gracious God, slow to anger, abound-
ing in love and faithfulness, maintaining love to thousands,
and forgiving wickedness, rebellion and sin. Yet he does not
leave the guilty unpunished; he punishes the children and
their children for the sin of the fathers to the third and
fourth generation.'

We should therefore be very careful not to extend the warning beyond the realm of idolatry into general sin.

4. The teaching in the second commandment is in the context of
the covenantal giving of the Law to the whole community of God's
people. Denis Sutherland speaks of the second commandment warning of punishment for *national* idolatry (italics mine) rather than
being directed to an individual. The same principle is contained in
Lamentations 5:7:

'Our fathers sinned and are no more and *we* bear their punishment'.

Similarly in Leviticus 26:40, confession for sin includes that of 'their fathers'. The principle is one of collective responsibility[19] and should not be applied in a purely individualistic sense.

It was precisely because people had begun to misapply this principle individually (they did the same thing in treating God's retribution as an excuse for personal revenge, see Matt. 5:38-42), that Ezekiel was told by the Spirit that the proverb 'the fathers have eaten sour grapes and the children's teeth are set on edge' should *no longer* be used in Israel (Ezek. 18:1-3ff). Jesus reinforces this in his dealings with the man born blind (John 9:1-3). The bystanders were convinced that the blindness must have had something to do with his own sin or that of his parents. Jesus says 'no'; as simple as that. Do we need more?

It has been argued that the man born blind was a special case (and perhaps the argument is used because the case runs clearly contrary to the theory of generational sin. We see things through the spectacles of our own subjective experience or preconceptions; sometimes looking for evidence to support our own position and discarding that which would appear to contradict it!). But in context it is clear that the stress was not upon 'this man'—as opposed to the rest of humanity—but rather 'this man' as opposed to his parents. The biblical principle remains constant that the man's blindness had no direct link with sin and that each is responsible for his own sin.[20]

There are of course characteristics which are genetically affected. Did Solomon, for example, inherit his propensity for women from his father? Was Jepthah affected by his illegitimacy as much as by his rejection by his brothers? But we are predestined rather than predetermined by the past.

As a sheep and cattle breeder I found that the characteristics which were carried in the genes affected not only the physical conformation of the young animal but also some of its attitudes. For instance, the calf of an aggressive bull was likely to be aggressive whatever treatment it received in adolescence. In the same way we, as humans, inherit not only physical attributes but also characteristics of nature and attitude. In this case we are very similar to animals and therefore the transmitting is 'genetic' rather than spiritual. To

deduce that there must be some spiritual cause for a son or daughter
to inherit certain attitudes from parents is to go beyond both Scripture and reason.

Just as individuals are affected by their genes, so the consequences
of social evil affect the next generation but the responsibility remains with the sinner.

> The soul who sins is the one who will die. The son will not
> share the guilt of the father, nor will the father share the
> guilt of the son. The righteousness of the righteous man
> will be credited to him, and the wickedness of the wicked
> will be charged against him. Ezekiel 18:20. See also Ro-
> mans 2:6; Psalm 62:12 *etc*.

Calvin states, 'It is inconsistent with the equity of the divine proce-
dure to punish the innocent for another's fault'[21] and surely this
principle lies at the very heart of the atonement. Jesus had to be
'made sin' for us (2Cor. 5:21). Our sins were laid upon him in such a
way that as substitute he became guilty: 'He was made a curse' (Gal.
3:13). Thus divine justice was exercised and divine mercy extended.
This is the very crux of the atonement and in the same way it is the
crux of our argument that God does not punish an individual for the
sins of another.

Augustine flirted with this teaching of generational sin but then
rejected it, and it has not since been seriously considered by Bible-
believing scholars. This may be partly at least because it could be
argued that if this principle applies then it must also apply to the
righteousness and faith of the believer with children inheriting their
parents' godliness, otherwise evil has an unfair advantage over good.
That there is some extending influence of holiness can be deduced
from 1 Corinthians 7:13-14 but it is clear that neither personal faith
and imputed righteousness nor personal guilt (as opposed to original sin) can be transmitted across the generations.

§

There are two further aspects of this teaching which require examination. The first is its close affinity with pagan Eastern religious teaching and the second is the effect upon those who come under its influence.

First, its affinity with Eastern religion. I received a report on Doctor Kenneth McAll, the author of *Healing the Family Tree*[22] couched in these terms:

> 'His thesis is that just as we inherit physical and emotional traits from our family—'he's just like his father'...'he gets that from his grandmother'...so also we inherit spiritual characteristics. If someone in our past has died traumatically, in war for example; if someone did not receive a proper funeral, committed in love; if there has been unforgiveness, or a failure to express true feelings; if someone has become involved in the occult—then, for any of these, or other reasons, it can cause problems for the living members of the family. *It would seem that the soul of the departed has not yet gone to the place appointed, and has remained 'earthbound' attaching to someone in the family*—until they hear the good news that Christ has died for the remission of sins. He is the Lamb of God who takes away the sin of the world'.

My first reaction was to recognise that the author is apparently speaking only of a pre-conversion condition and therefore is presenting very different teaching to others on generational sin. My second reaction was to show the passage to a former missionary in Bhutan with much experience of Eastern religion. His comment was: 'That is pure (*sic*) Buddhism'. He went on to give a horrific account of a family praying at the deathbed of their daughter—not for her physical or spiritual wellbeing but rather that her spirit would not remain earthbound and consequently affect any of them!

The second and perhaps more important aspect is the pastoral impact upon Christians who come under condemnation by the insensitive application of this doctrine of generational sin. I am aware that it is only too easy to select case histories to support one's own position, but the two quoted below are not isolated and represent dangers in particular areas.

I know a family whose surname featured among the defeated clans at Culloden who were constantly being told that they had to be delivered from 'the spirit of Culloden' (seen as defeat and depression). The effect on that family of a deepening depression can easily be imagined. Only after years of pain did the family move to a Church where the whole counsel of God is preached and where they are all now serving and rejoicing in the Lord.

Another single mother had many deep problems and had undergone 'deliverance ministry' where it was claimed various spirits had been cast out. The result was a fear that there were still more such spirits lurking in her background so that she could never enter into the peace of the finished work of the Cross. The 'can of worms' seemed bottomless until covered by faith in the blood of Jesus.

# VI

# Can Christians be Demonised?

Can a true child of God be *occupied,* as opposed to *attacked,* by an evil or unclean spirit? The question arises because Christians still have problems with, and clearly are affected by, evil. Some of these problems are at least partly attributable to background or early life. The issue therefore is where these problems originate so that they can be helped and solved. It would seem that there are three possible answers to the question.

### The first possible answer: sin in the believer
The long-held view of orthodox Christianity seems to me to be as follows. Sin is dead in the believer who has died to sin in Christ whose death has struck at the very root of sin (Rom. 6). Nevertheless, there is a residue or sediment upon which Satan and his forces may work from outside in order to stir up a situation contrary both to the will of God and the genuine inner desire of the Christian (Rom. 7).

A helpful illustration can be taken from wine-making where the 'lees'[23] which is the sediment at the bottom of the container, is chemically dead but yet can cloud the wine if shaken. Clearly on this view, Christians are garrisoned by the Holy Spirit but must enter into that safety by faith: they are indeed 'come to fullness, in Christ' (Col. 2:10) and have entered the staggering reality stated in Hebrews 10:14: 'Because by one sacrifice He (Christ) has made perfect for ever those who are being made perfect'. Do we take this entering into fullness and being made perfect or mature purely in the realm of the forensic? Is there nothing of applied reality in it? The Scripture is clear that there must be more. There must be spiritual reality in the Christian's daily living. Indeed the context of Hebrews 10:14 is one of spiritual warfare where the Warrior Priest waits for his enemies to be put under his feet.

Is there not an analogy here with us? This is surely highly practical. We have entered by faith into the gift of the fullness of Christ. That does not, of course, mean that we are now perfect. But it does imply we truly are partakers of the fullness of Christ as well as ever progressing more deeply into that fullness in a way that radically transforms us. We are *to be* what we *are*.

To admit that demons could enter or re-enter those who have come to fullness in Christ is surely perilously close to blasphemy. All analogies are bound to be limited but the parable of the tramp makes the point of our humanity (though regenerate) so often failing to possess that which is ours by right of the Cross. The tramp had been befriended by a millionaire and given the freedom of his house. He would stay for a while putting his old life behind him until the pull of the road became too strong and he reverted to being a tramp again, so letting his friend down again and again. Picked up by the police on one occasion he was informed by the millionaire's solicitor that he had inherited all the riches of his benefactor. Stunned, he walked around the magnificent mansion saying to himself, 'I spurned all his love but now it is mine, all mine!' But he has been living in a shed at the bottom of the garden ever since...

We need to enter our inheritance by faith. We need to recognise that in Christ all things are ours. We are wise therefore to dwell upon the inheritance rather than look for snakes in the garden!

## The second possible answer: Satan and his demons attacking the believer from outside

The Christian is called upon to take up the whole armour of God provided to ward off the attacks of Satan and his demons. There would be little point in providing or wearing the armour if the enemy were already inside! Although this powerful implication of the provision of the armour of God clearly precludes the third answer, we must now examine it more fully.

## The third possible answer: demons attacking from within

To help consideration of the third possibility let us try to maintain the unity of the Spirit with others without compromising the truth. Denis Sutherland has some helpful suggestions here. First, we must first turn to Scripture to look for a clear statement. However, there is no passage of Scripture which unequivocally states that a Christian can or cannot be occupied by a demon.

Second, we can think theologically on the basis of Scripture and the easier our position lies with the Scriptural witness the better it will be. Unfortunately neither side finds the position of the other, even when fully explained, convincing, and both tend to think that the opposite camp is failing to draw legitimate conclusions from the biblical data. Parabolic analogies fail to convince since not everything in the parable will necessarily correspond in full to the real life situation.

Third, we are left with experience, but this too is inconclusive. Both sides will adduce examples in support of their own position and produce examples of disasters they allege were caused by adopting the other position. Anecdotes are problematical since selectivity and misinterpretation can easily occur and cross-checking is rarely possible.

Assuming that all are reasoning and acting in good faith and that any manifestations are not satanic deception in this controversial area, there are three possibilities:

- The victim is a Christian and the demonic activity is external but the helper thinks it is internal. In such a case God may in grace ignore the error of the helper and liberate the victim.
- The victim only appears to be a Christian but is not truly indwelt by the Spirit of Christ.
- The victim is indeed a Christian and is inhabited by a demon or demons.

I find such an approach attractive but believe that the third position quoted above cannot be in line with Scripture and should be rejected for the following reasons, four of which are phrased in the form of questions.

*Reason one*—Although it is an argument from silence, we may ask why Scripture has no record of a Christian being demonised or delivered from demons. Some will quote the case of Peter in Matthew 16:23: 'Jesus said to Peter, "Get behind me Satan..."' But it clearly makes more sense to understand the voice and activity of Satan as coming from outside, and simply using Peter's ignorance of the meaning of the Cross. The phrase, 'Satan has put it in your heart,' conjures up a picture of the chef putting poison in the pudding—but the chef is not inside the pudding! Others may point to Simon Magi in Acts 8 but his 'believism' clearly lacked the vital spark of regeneration.

*Reason two*—Why is it the teaching of the Epistles (the Apostle's Doctrine where we should expect to find instructions to the Church) that we should look by faith to what we are in Christ rather than to look inside for contrary forces? This is overwhelmingly the consistent New Testament emphasis.

*Reason three*—Why is the casting out of demons restricted in the Scriptures to unbelieving Jews and Gentiles? It may be argued that the Jews of Jesus' day were the people of God. Such an argument fails on several counts. It makes no distinction between nominal and genuine believers. For example, although the woman in Luke 13 is described as 'a daughter of Abraham' yet Scripture makes it clear that not all the daughters or sons of the man of faith were the children of God by faith.[24] Thus it weakens the dynamic of the effect of Pentecost when the Spirit was given to apply the work of Christ to human hearts and lives.

*Reason four*—Why is the armour provided by God if the enemy can be within? There is a saying about stable doors being shut after the horse has left!

*Reason five*—Satan is normally a legalist and he and his demons use the good Law of God for their nefarious purposes. Luther repulsed the attacks of Satan with the simple statement 'I am baptised'. The effectiveness of this indicates that the Scriptural teaching is indeed that demons have no legal right in the life of believers, whose legal position is sealed by baptism.

*Reason six*—Much emphasis is placed by those involved in the deliverance ministry upon such phrases as 'the spirit of lust, hate *etc.*,' but no reference to the details of any particular demon are given in Scripture and, perhaps surprisingly, the ordinary cases of possession of a person by a demon in the New Testament do not result in him being led so far astray as to do things which are morally reprehensible.[25] Satan certainly leads morally astray but paradoxically the demons do not seem to do so. Certainly they try to influence people to sin 'from without'[26] but this is very different from an inner malign presence causing an attitude.

§

This clearly raises an issue which we have looked at before: If possessing demons do not necessarily compel us to sin, and demonic activity can be non-moral, then what of the casting out of such spirits claimed to be 'the spirit of lust, envy, *etc.*'?

By encouraging the experience of what we may call a counterfeit deliverance it may be that Satan gains access to attack a soul by casting doubts on the completeness of the work of Christ. He may produce evidence of the healing either of the disease or of the symptoms (there is a major difference between the two) in order to reinforce his lie. Let me illustrate what I mean by quoting, with permission, part of a letter from a woman who had had this teaching thrust upon her in an unbalanced and unbiblical way.

'Christians are led to believe that they really can be possessed. This leads to a very unhealthy state in which they are on constant watch to see what demons are lurking in their own soul and are equally vigilant about all those thought to be inhabiting their fellow Christians. This has the effect of destroying trust and fellowship between Christians and removes the emphasis of their life from service to the pursuit of imaginary demons within—or in others.'

I am happy to record that woman is now set free through faith in Christ's complete work, brought home to her by the Word and the love of her new congregation.

I would stress yet again the effect of this feature of mutual distrust. In the eyes of many who hold this doctrine, a very high percentage of us who hold to the reformed faith would be accused of being occupied by a religious spirit or of having the same pharisaic spirit which caused so much opposition to Jesus when he was on earth. Fellowship under those circumstances becomes difficult if not impossible. It can divide not only Churches but even Christian families.

§

We started by stressing that we are not dealing here merely with a matter of spiritual and intellectual understanding of a doctrine but with an issue whose pastoral implications are of immense importance. There are two.

First, the teaching of this third possible answer that demons attack from within, applied in an unbalanced way, can be highly unsettling to sensitive leaders. We begin to wonder if we have really missed out on something of real spiritual importance. (Note that this is the attraction of the Masonic Order where extra, secret knowledge is promised). This may lead to a deep disturbance of spirit which the accuser of the brethren will use to bring much self-condemnation, with resultant bondage of spirit.

Second, it can lead our people into an unhealthy obsession with the whole subject. We all know how attractive the occult can be with its fascination with things hidden; could it be that 'deep secrets of Satan' (Rev. 2:24) is that fascination (that very word rings alarm bells in my spirit) in the Church with the unrevealed and exciting secret areas of the psyche which then becomes 'the Christian occult'. My wife, who has great spiritual wisdom and discernment, came out with this little jingle:

> Could concentration on demons be
> The oldest form of idolatrie?

I think that came from God; certainly there is real truth there.

Nigel Wright recognises this progression from interest to fascination and puts it in these words:

> 'While we should acknowledge the existence of Satan and evil spirits—*ie* believe that they exist—we should not 'believe in' these powers. For to believe in someone or something implies not only an acknowledgement that they exist but also carries overtones of faith and trust'.[27]

Let us be aware too, that, perhaps especially in this area, the line between truth and error is an extremely fine one. Some of the methods used today in 'faith healing' and which may have crept into the Church are those which stem from and are used by Voodoo, witch doctors and certain eastern mystics. The techniques of visualisation and certain aspects of healing of the memories owe more to these sources than to the Christ of the Scriptures.

Does this automatically make them taboo or can the method, although in itself suspect, be used by Christ without compromise? Certainly Joseph claimed to use suspect divination techniques (Gen. 44:5) and the Lord Jesus made use of some strange methods on occasions.[28] There are no rigid rules. How we need that gracious discernment of the spirits!

# VII

# The All-Sufficiency of Christ

In the realm of physical medicine, prevention is recognised as being more important than cure. The Old Testament teaching on physical health, with its underlying principles for spiritual health, concentrates almost exclusively upon prevention. Surely we need to emphasise the positive aspects of the Gospel of whole salvation rather than dwell upon cures for those who have ignored the health rules. I conclude this booklet with two points in this connection.

First: we need to stress the necessity of a 'sound' conversion—not the mere submission to a simplistic view of salvation but a radical change of ownership and human nature. The work of counselling a new Christian is like that of a midwife entering into the very pangs of childbirth (Gal. 4:19), and should never be glib or superficial. Perhaps the old phrase 'I renounce the devil and all his works' should be reintroduced, especially where some contact with the occult may have taken place.

I sat at the front of Gilcomston South Church after preaching at the evening service. A Christian girl whom I had known for years and who had been involved with the occult came to speak with me. After some time I told her that she had to say those words, and mean them! We sat for three quarters of an hour as my tea got cold until eventually her resistance was broken down as many were praying. She spoke out the words from the heart and knew an immediate release. The deliverance came through the power of the Holy Spirit enabling her to use her God-given will. 'Work out your own salvation...for God is at work in you' (Phil. 2:12f).

Finally, we need to appreciate that only a biblical understanding of sin, its residue and consequences, of Satan and his devices, and of the dynamic of the Gospel of the Cross will enable Christians to enter into the assured peace and ultimate victory of Christ in times of spiritual and moral attack. My plea to those who are struggling with fears and suspicions about evil spirits is to concentrate upon *holiness* before *wholeness*. Take your eyes off the devil and yourself and your past in unhealthy introspection and fix them firmly upon the Cross and the risen Lord.

I say 'the Cross' advisedly because it is Christ and him crucified and risen who alone gives the victory over Satan today having deci-

sively defeated him by going through death. He shared our humanity so that by his death he might destroy him who holds the power of
death, that is the Devil, and set free those who all their lives were
held in slavery by their fear of death (Heb. 2:14-15). He, having
disarmed the powers and authorities, made a public spectacle of
them, triumphing over them by the Cross (Col. 2:15).

If, as Christians, we are rooted and grounded in Christ and have
entered fully into all that is ours as a result of the finished work of
Christ on the Cross, ratified by the resurrection and confirmed by
the Holy Spirit, then we can indeed face our fierce accuser with
confidence and resist the Devil who goes around like a roaring lion
with the simple word, 'Jesus died; and rose again'.

There is a picture in Isaiah 14:3ff of those who are released from
bondage 'taking up a taunt' against the oppressor. I am not suggest-
ing that we should all take this literally but were we standing firm
in Christ that would be closer to our attitude to Satan than the
present state of many of ignorance or cringing fear.

*'Thanks be to God who gives us the victory in Jesus Christ'.*

# Notes

1    Overseas Missionary Fellowship, *Quarterly Prayer News*, Sep-
     tember 1994.
2    This is not to deny that the devil is unquestionably responsible
     for much trouble and heartache in believers' lives. Rather am I
     emphasising the responsibility each of us carries before our
     God.
3    Note, however, that in Scripture there are only three direct
     encounters with Satan: in Genesis 3, Job 1 and Matthew 4. His
     unseen influence is nevertheless constantly implied and taught.
4    *Diakrisis* is used only in 1 Corinthians 12:10; Romans 14:1 and
     Hebrews 5:14.
5    *Collected Writings of William Still,* Vol.2, Edinburgh, Rutherford
     House, 1994, pages 2ff.
6    C. S. Lewis, *Mere Christianity*, Book 2, Collins, 1965, ch. two.

7    See Matthew 15:16ff; Luke 24:45; Mark 12:33 *et al.*

8    Romans 12:2; 1Corinthians 14:20; Colossians 1:9; Philippians 4:7, *et al.*

9    Revelation 13:18.

10   Proverbs 23:7 AV; Mark 7:15, 21ff.

11   1 Corinthians 2:16; Philippians 2:5 and Romans 8:27.

12   See pages 18f.

13   For example, see Francis McNutt, *Healing,* Hodder & Stoughton, 1989.

14   See Colossians 4:14; 1 Timothy 5:23 *et al.*

15   Dr Tom Brown, Consultant Psychiatrist, writing to a colleague on this subject, endorsed this view.

16   Genesis 1:28; Psalm 8:6; Hebrews 2:5-18.

17   Peter Horrobin, *Healing through Deliverance*, Sovereign World, 1991.

18   By this is meant that there are areas of specific weakness and susceptibility to sin which can be inherited. For example, a tendency towards alcoholism or womanising may run in a family; nevertheless, scripture teaches that the responsibility for individual sins firmly rests with each person.(Author's note)

19   *Cf.* Nehemiah 1:6f; Daniel 9:5f.

20   Deuteronomy 24:16; Romans 14:12, *et al.*

21   John Calvin, *Institutes*, II, 8, 19.

22   Kenneth McAll, *Healing the Family Tree*, Sheldon Press (SPCK) 1986, is quoted by Rev. David Lunan in Carberry News, Summer 1994.

23   See Isaiah 25:2 (AV); Jeremiah 48:11(AV).

24   John 1:12; Romans 2:28f.

25   See J.Michl, art., 'Demon', in J. B. Bauer, *Enclyclopaedia of Biblical Theology*, Sheed & Ward, 1992.

26   1Timothy 4:1-3; 1John 4:6; *et al.*

27   Nigel Wright, *The Fair Face of Evil, Putting the power of darkness in its place*, Marshall-Pickering, 1989.

28   See Mark 7:33; 8:23; John 9:6.